Excel

A Step-by-Step Guide with Practical Examples to Master Excel's Basics, Functions, Formulas, Tables, and Charts

Jack A. Finke

ISBN-13: 979-8868339585

DEDICATION

To every one of my readers!

TABLE OF CONTENT

Introduction

Mastering Excel is a valuable skill that can greatly enhance your productivity and effectiveness in today's data-driven world. Whether you're a student, professional, or simply someone looking to improve their organizational abilities, learning Excel is a wise investment of your time. In this section, we will explore the fundamental concepts of Excel and provide beginners with a solid foundation to build upon.

Excel is a powerful spreadsheet program developed by Microsoft. It allows users to manipulate, analyze, and visualize data in a structured format. From creating simple tables to performing complex calculations, Excel offers a wide range of features that can help you streamline your work and make informed decisions. With its intuitive design and user-friendly interface design, Excel is accessible to users of all skill levels.

One of the key features of Excel is its ability to organize data in a tabular format. You can create tables to store and categorize information, making it easier to manage and retrieve data when needed. Excel also offers a variety of formatting options to customize the appearance of your tables, such as adjusting borders, colors, and font styles. This allows you to present your data in a visually appealing manner, making it easier to interpret and understand.

In addition to organizing data, Excel provides powerful tools for performing analysis and calculations. You can use functions and formulas to automate calculations, saving you time and effort. Whether you need to calculate averages, totals, or perform more complex mathematical operations, Excel has you covered. Its extensive library of built-in functions allows you to perform a wide range of operations without the need for complex mathematical equations.

Graphs and charts are another powerful feature of Excel. They allow you to visualize your data in a meaningful way, enabling you to identify patterns, trends, and relationships. With just a few clicks, you can create professional-looking graphs and charts that highlight the key insights from your data. Whether you need to create a pie chart, line graph, or bar chart, Excel provides a wide range of options to choose from.

Collaboration is made easy with Excel's sharing and collaboration features. You can share your Excel files with others, allowing them to comment on, edit, and view your work. This makes it easier to work on group projects, share data with clients, or collaborate with colleagues. Excel also offers version control, so you can track changes and restore previous versions if needed.

Lastly, Excel is a versatile tool that can be customized to suit your specific needs. With its extensive range of options and features, you can tailor Excel to match your preferences and workflow. From adding custom shortcuts to creating macros, Excel allows you to personalize your experience and work more efficiently.

In a nutshell, learning Excel is a valuable skill that can open up a world of possibilities. Whether you're organizing information, analyzing business data, or managing personal finances, Excel can make your work easier. By understanding the fundamental concepts of Excel and practicing its features, beginners can lay a solid foundation for their Excel journey. So, don't hesitate to dive into the world of Excel and unlock its full potential.

Chapter 1: Getting Started with Microsoft Excel

Microsoft Excel is a popular piece of software included in the Microsoft Office suite. It serves as a spreadsheet tool that enables users to store and analyze numerical data.

Here, we present the key functionalities of MS Excel, accompanied by a general guide on its usage, advantages, and other significant components.

1.1 Defining Microsoft Excel

Microsoft Excel is a powerful piece of software developed and released by Microsoft that allows users to input data in tabular format. It provides a convenient way to analyze data in a spreadsheet. It is widely used for organizing and analyzing data, creating charts and graphs, and performing financial calculations. Excel is known for its user-friendly interface, which allows users to easily enter data and perform complex calculations using formulas and functions.

1.2 A Brief History of MS Excel

In its early days, Excel was not the dominant tool it is now. Its roots can be traced back to the 1980s, when a group of Microsoft developers embarked on a mission to develop software that could effectively handle financial data. They wanted to create a program that would allow users to organize, analyze, and visualize data in a way that was intuitive and user-friendly.

The result of their efforts was the birth of Excel. Released in 1985, it quickly gained popularity among businesses and individuals alike. Its ability to handle complex calculations and create visually appealing charts and graphs made it an indispensable tool for professionals in various industries.

Over the years, Excel continued to evolve and improve. New features were added, making it even more versatile and powerful. The introduction of macros allowed users to automate repetitive tasks, saving them time and effort. The addition of pivot tables made it easier to summarize and analyze large amounts of data.

Perhaps one of the most significant milestones in Excel's history was the introduction of Excel for Windows in 1987. This version of the software was optimized for the Windows operating system, taking full advantage of its graphical user interface. It was a game-changer, propelling Excel to new heights of success and cementing its place as the go-to spreadsheet program.

Today, Excel remains an integral part of Microsoft's Office suite, and its impact on the business world cannot be overstated. From financial modeling and data analysis to project management and inventory tracking, Excel is used in a wide range of applications. Its versatility and ease of use have made it an essential tool for professionals across industries.

Looking ahead, the future of Excel is bright. Microsoft continues to invest in its development, adding new features and functionalities to keep up with the ever-changing needs of its users. With the rise of data-driven decision-making, the demand for tools like Excel is only expected to grow.

1.3 Launching Excel for the First Time

To access Microsoft Excel on your computer for the first time, here's what you need to do:

- Start by clicking on the "Start" button located at the bottom left corner of your screen. This will open the Start menu, where you'll find a list of all the applications installed on your computer.
- Look for the "Microsoft Office" folder within the Start menu. Click on it to expand the folder and reveal a list of all the Microsoft Office applications available to you.
- Among the list of applications, you'll find "Excel." Click on it to launch the program. Alternatively, you can use the search bar at the top of the Start menu and type "Excel" to quickly locate and launch the application.
- Once you've clicked on Excel, a new window will appear, presenting you with a blank workbook. This is where the magic happens!

1.4 What are a Cell and a Cell Address?

In the world of spreadsheets, a cell is the building block. It takes the form of a table, with rows and columns defining its structure. At the juncture of these rows and columns, we find rectangular boxes that represent cells.

To identify and locate a specific cell, we use its cell address. This address serves as the cell's name, allowing us to refer to it easily. For instance, if we want to access the cell in column D of row 9, we would refer to the cell address as D9.

1.5 What Can Microsoft Excel Do?

Excel offers a wide range of features and tools that assist users in effectively organizing, managing, analyzing, and visualizing data. Professionals worldwide rely on Excel due to its extensive capabilities. Here are some of the key features and tools that make Microsoft Excel a preferred choice:

- In Excel, you can perform various calculations like averaging, adding, finding low, median, or high values, counting cells with numbers, and multiplying cells for product calculation.
- You can also remove extra white space and truncate numbers to remove fractions.

- Collaborating with others is easy, as you can share workbooks in real-time.
- Excel learns your usage patterns over time to organize data and save time.
- Another useful feature is the ability to add data from a photo, which eliminates the need for manual entry.
- Excel works seamlessly across web, desktop, and mobile devices.
- PivotTables in Excel allow for the analysis and summarization of datasets, enabling better comparisons and understanding of revenue sources.
- You can also import financial transactions to organize and review your financial information, gaining insights for informed decision-making.

1.6 Common Use Case for Microsoft Excel

Excel is a versatile tool that finds applications in various professions and industries. Its uses include:

- Inputting and storing data
- Gathering, organizing, and validating business data
- Analyzing data
- Presenting data visually
- Managing accounting and budgeting tasks
- Generating reports based on data
- Project management
- Performance reporting

- Streamlining administrative or managerial tasks
- Managing accounts or operations
- Creating calendars or schedules
- Forecasting future trends.

1.7 Advantages of Working with MS Excel

Learning and working with Microsoft Excel offers several benefits. Here are some of its benefits:

Improve Your Data Organization Skills

In today's data-driven world, Excel is the go-to tool for organizing vast amounts of information. With a solid understanding of Excel, you can effectively structure and manage raw data in ways that are valuable for your company. Excel's advanced features provide various sorting options, making it easier to analyze numbers and perform necessary calculations.

Boost Your Efficiency at Work

Knowing Excel functions, tools, and shortcuts can significantly speed up your tasks. One particularly time-saving feature is macros, which automate repetitive tasks and data manipulations. You don't need coding knowledge to create macros, and they can save you hours of work in just minutes.

Enhance Your Value to the Organization

Having Excel skills sets you apart as a valuable employee and increases your chances of advancing in your career. By continuously improving your efficiency and expanding your knowledge of Excel functions, you demonstrate your dedication to the company's success. This makes you less likely to be replaced by others with more advanced skills.

Collaborates Effectively with Others

Excel is a powerful collaboration tool that allows multiple people to work on the same worksheet or workbook simultaneously. Real-time updates ensure that everyone involved in a project is aware of any changes made to the spreadsheet. These streamlines work processes and speeds up completion time.

Optimize Your Organization's Resources

Excel proficiency is an excellent way to make the most of your company's assets. By utilizing this software effectively, you can unlock the full potential of other underutilized resources within the organization.

Simplify Your Job

As you become more proficient in Excel, you'll find that navigating the application and performing job-related tasks become effortless. Moreover, the shortcuts and features you learn in Excel often apply to other Microsoft 365 products, making your workflow smoother and allowing you to reuse spreadsheet data in other programs.

Presents Data Findings Visually

Sharing data findings with colleagues or stakeholders often requires effective data visualization. Excel offers a range of visualization options, including graphs and charts, which help convey information in a visually appealing and accessible way. Excel's regular updates introduce even better visualization features, such as sunburst diagrams and map charts.

Relieves IT Support Burden

Employees who lack Excel skills can burden the IT support team, as they often require individual training. This can distract IT personnel from more critical tasks, like security maintenance and system upgrades. By equipping employees with advanced Excel skills, organizations can alleviate this strain on the IT department.

Increase Your Earning Potential

Proficiency in Excel opens up job opportunities and can lead to higher starting salaries. Employers consider Excel expertise a valuable transferable skill, making you a desirable candidate for many positions. The more you know about Excel, the greater your professional options and earning potential.

Efficient Expense Tracking

Excel offers built-in templates and tools for tracking business expenses. The expense report template, for example, allows users to organize expense data into customizable columns and labels. Additionally, Excel provides manual options for creating expense reports tailored to specific budgeting needs.

Chapter 2: Setting up MS Excel on Your Device

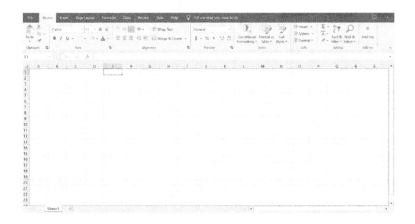

2.1 Downloading Excel on Desktop and Mobile Devices

If you're interested in getting Microsoft Excel on your tablet, phone, or computer, there are a few options available. Firstly, although MS Excel for computers is only available as part of the Microsoft Office 365 package, you can download Excel separately for free on Android and iPhone devices. Secondly, it's important to note that a Microsoft account is required to purchase and use Office 365 on a computer. If you have Office 365 installed but Excel is missing, simply reinstalling the software may do the trick. In this section, we will guide you through the process of downloading Microsoft Excel on your Android, iPad, iPhone, Mac, or Windows device.

2.1.1 How to Use Office 365 on Your Desktop

Using Office 365 on your desktop is a straightforward process. Here's a step-by-step guide to help you get started:

- Purchase an Office 365 subscription. To download Microsoft Excel for long-term use, you must first buy an Office 365 subscription. Make sure you have a Microsoft account to complete the purchase. Alternatively, you can opt for a free trial of Office 365 for a month.

- Visit office.com/myaccount/ in your web browser. Open your web browser and go to office.com/myaccount/. If you're already logged in, this will take you to your Office subscription page. If not, enter your email address and password when prompted.

- Click on "Install Office." On the page, locate and click on the "Install Office" button. It's situated on the right side and is colored blue. You'll find it next to your active subscription. This action will trigger a pop-up window.

- Click on "Install." Within the pop-up window, click on the "Install" button. You'll find it at the bottom-right corner. If necessary, you can modify the language and version of Office by using the drop-down menu. Afterward, the setup file will start downloading, and depending on your browser settings, you may need to select a save location or confirm the download.

- Install Office 365. The installation process for Office 365 varies depending on your computer's operating system. Here's what you should do:

a) Windows: Once the setup file is downloaded, double-click it and select "Yes" when prompted. Wait for the installation to complete, and when prompted, click "Close" to finalize the installation.
b) Mac: Double-click the setup file and click "Continue" → "Continue" → "Agree" → "Continue" → "Install". Enter your Mac's password and click "Install Software". Finally, click "Close" when prompted.

- Open Excel. After successfully installing Office 365, you can access Microsoft Excel. It comes bundled with every version of Office 365. Here's how to find it:

a) Windows: Click on the Start button and type "excel" in the search bar. The Excel icon will appear at the top of the Start menu.
b) Mac: Click on Spotlight and type "Excel." Excel will appear at the top of the search results.

- You're now ready to use Excel!

2.1.2 Exploring the Desktop Free Trial Option

To try Office 365 for free:

- Visit the Office website in your computer's web browser.
- Click "Try 1 month free" on the left side of the page.
- Sign in to your Microsoft account with your email address and password.
- Provide a payment method to start the free trial. You can cancel before the trial ends if you don't want to be charged.
- Select a payment method and enter the required information.
- Confirm your information and click "Subscribe" at the bottom of the page.
- Click "Install" to download the setup to your computer.

- Install Office 365 by following the on-screen instructions. The process may vary depending on your operating system.

- If you decide not to continue with the subscription, remember to cancel before the trial period ends. You can do this by visiting the Microsoft account services page, clicking "Payment & billing" under the "Office 365" section, and selecting "Cancel." Confirm the cancellation when prompted.

2.1.3 Using Excel on Your Android Device

- To get started with Microsoft Excel on your Android device, open the Google Play Store. Simply tap on the Play Store app icon, which you can find as a multicolored triangle on a white background.

- Once you're in the Google Play Store, locate the search bar at the top of the screen. Tap on it, and your Android's on-screen keyboard will appear.

- Now, it's time to find the Excel app. Type the word "excel" into the search bar, and you will see a drop-down menu with options. Look for Microsoft Excel, which is represented by a green-and-white Excel icon, and tap on it. This will take you to the Microsoft Excel page.

- On the Excel page, you will see an option that says "INSTALL." Tap on it, and the app will start downloading onto your Android device. If you are asked to accept any prompts, go ahead and do so to initiate the download.

- Once the download is complete, open the Microsoft Excel app. You can do this by tapping on the "OPEN" button within the Google Play Store or by locating the app icon in your app drawer.

Remember, in order to use Microsoft Excel, you will need to log into a Microsoft account. This will allow you to access and utilize the app's features.

2.1.4 Using Excel on Your iPad or iPhone Devices

To access Microsoft Excel on your iPad or iPhone, follow these simple steps:

- Launch the App Store by tapping on the App Store icon, which is a white "A" on a light-blue background.
- Look for the search function by tapping on the magnifying glass-shaped icon located in the bottom-right corner of the screen.
- In the search bar, type "excel" and tap on the "search" button. This will display a list of apps related to Excel.
- Find the official Microsoft Excel app and tap on it to select it. Make sure it is developed by Microsoft Corporation.

- To download the app, tap on the "GET" button located below the Microsoft Excel title. If you have previously downloaded Excel, you may see a cloud icon instead.
- Confirm your purchase by following the prompts. Depending on your device or settings, you may need to use your Apple ID password, Touch ID, or Face ID to verify the purchase.
- Once the installation is complete, open the Microsoft Excel app either from the App Store or by locating the app icon on your home screen.
- You will be prompted to log into a Microsoft account in order to begin using the app. Once you're logged in, you can start creating spreadsheets on your iPad or iPhone.

2.2 Is it Necessary to Spend Money on Microsoft 365?

Is it really necessary to shell out money for Microsoft 365? Well, not exactly. You have two options here: either pay for Microsoft 365 or utilize the free Microsoft 365 webapps. Each option comes with its own perks.

Paying for Microsoft 365 grants you access to installed software, webapps, regular updates, and a generous 1TB of online storage. The subscription fee is quite reasonable, but if you decide to cancel, you'll lose access to the tools you rely on. Alternatively, you could opt for Office Home & Student 2021, but it lacks the most enticing features of Microsoft 365.

On the other hand, using the free Microsoft 365 webapps won't cost you a penny and allows you to work from anywhere. However, keep in mind that these webapps are not as robust as their installed counterparts, and your OneDrive storage is limited to a mere 5GB. Plus, if your internet connection goes down, you'll be forced to put your work on hold.

2.3 Understanding Extensions in Microsoft Excel

Every tool or piece of software has its own way of saving files, and these methods are only compatible with that particular tool or piece of software. Microsoft Excel is a widely used tool that has undergone numerous upgrades, resulting in the addition of new file extensions. File extensions serve to indicate the type of file. Typically, a suffix is added at the end of a file name, consisting of two or four characters. The extension is separated from the file name by a dot. For example, in the file name "Excel.docx," ".docx" is the file extension, while "Excel" is the file name.

Understanding file extensions is important because they provide information about the file type. To open a file, you need to know its file type in order to have the appropriate software. Additionally, you may need to manage saved files in directories using various formats, such as macro-enabled files or template files. Excel file extensions provide information on whether the file is formatted in XML or binary, whether it is a template, whether it contains macros or VBA code, and whether it is saved in the latest version.

To view file extensions in Excel, click on the "File" option in the menu. Then, choose "Save As" and select the file type dropdown menu located under the file name box.

Each file type will have a descriptive name that helps you understand its corresponding file extension.

2.3.1 How to Locate Your Excel File Extensions

If you're unsure where to find the file formats, simply open the save dialog box. In the "Save as type" section, you'll find a list of all the available file formats on your system. The file extension "*.xlsx" is used to identify Excel workbooks.

2.3.2 Different Versions of Excel and Their Corresponding File Extensions

Different versions of Excel use different file extensions to indicate the format in which the worksheet was saved. Here are some examples:

- ".xlt" → Excel 97-2003 template
- ".xls" → Excel 97-2003
- ".xls" → Microsoft Excel 5.0/95 Workbook
- ".xml" → XML Spreadsheet 2003
- ".xlw" → Excel 4.0
- ".xlam" → Excel 97-2003 Add-in
- ".xlr" → Microsoft Works

Before Excel 2007, the default file extension used for all versions of Excel was *.xls. However, starting with Excel 2007, the default file extension became *.xlsx.

2.3.3 Extensions: Considerations to Keep in Mind

- It is important to approach the extension of an Excel file with patience and care.
- The size of the file can be reduced by up to 50% by utilizing the Excel Binary Workbook.
- Macros are associated with the "XLSM" extension type.
- The "CSV" file extension is not meant for working in Excel, as it is primarily used for data storage and can also help reduce file size.

Chapter 3: The Excel User Interface

In Excel spreadsheets, the user interface consists of more than just a rectangular grid of columns and rows. Here are the main components of the interface:

3.1 Top-Side Components

In the upper part of the Excel user interface, you will find several components that play a crucial role in your interaction with the software. These elements are designed to provide you with easy access to various functions and features. Here's a few:

3.1.1 Title Bar

The title bar is the area at the top of the Excel window that displays the name of the workbook. By default, a new workbook is named Book1, and subsequent workbooks are named Book2, Book3, and so on. However, once you save the workbook, the title bar will be updated to show the filename you chose for the Excel file.

3.1.2 Quick Access Toolbar

The Quick Access Toolbar is a handy feature found in the top left-side area of your display. It includes frequently used icons for easy access. In Excel 2007, you can find it on the right side of the Office button. In versions starting with Excel 2010, it is located above the Home and File tabs. By default, the toolbar contains icons for Save, Repeat, and Undo. If you want to customize it, simply click on the tiny down-arrow at the right end of the toolbar to open a customization dialog box.

3.2 Ribbon Components

3.2.1 Ribbon Tabs

Ribbon tabs are the main menu items located at the top. These include formulas, page layout, insert, home, and more. The available options may vary depending on the context. To access various features in Excel, simply click on any of these tabs. Each tab corresponds to a different ribbon.

3.2.2 Ribbon

The Ribbon is essentially a collection of Excel features organized into groups that align with the ribbon tabs. For instance, the Home ribbon is divided into groups such as Number, Alignment, Font, Clipboard, and more. Each group contains icons representing specific Excel capabilities. For instance, if you would like to center the content of a cell in your worksheet, click on the desired cell before clicking on the center icon found in the Alignment group on the Home ribbon.

Similarly, you can merge two adjacent cells by highlighting them and selecting Home > Alignment | Merge & Center. This combines the cells and centers any content placed in the merged cell. Furthermore, you can insert, delete, and format columns, rows, cells, and worksheets using Home > Cells.

In addition, there are shortcuts available for certain icons. For instance, to center the contents of a cell, you can click on the cell and then press Ctrl-E.

3.3 Icons

Icons serve a purpose in software interfaces. You can hover your mouse over an icon to see a tooltip with information about its function. On a ribbon, some groups have a small arrow next to their name. Clicking this arrow opens a dialog box with various options. For example, clicking the arrow next to the Font group on the Home ribbon brings up tabs like Border, Font, Alignment, Number, etc. Each tab offers different formatting options for the selected cells. To display numbers with three decimal places, you would select the Number tab, choose the Number option, and enter "3" in the decimal places box.

Within a group, some icons have a small downward arrow. Clicking this arrow reveals a vertical list of options. For instance, clicking the Insert icon in the Cells group on the Home ribbon presents choices like Insert Sheet..., Insert Sheet Columns, Insert Sheet Rows, and Insert Cells.

Certain groups feature scrollable drop-down lists with a downward arrow. Clicking the arrow next to the Font drop-down list in the Font group on the Home ribbon displays a list of available fonts (Times New Roman, Arial, etc.) that you can choose from.

3.4 Office Button and File Ribbon

The Office Button is an essential feature in the Excel 2007 interface. It can be found in the upper left corner and offers convenient access to important functions like opening, saving, and printing workbooks. Upon clicking the Office button, a menu will appear, giving you several options to choose from. One of these options is Excel Options, which, when clicked, opens a dialog box where you can modify various configuration settings.

Furthermore, Excel 2010 and later versions have replaced the Office button with the File tab. The File tab, situated to the left of the Home tab, serves the same purpose as the Office Button, granting users access to the same functionalities.

3.5 Components Underneath the Ribbon

3.5.1 Name Box

The Name Box is where you can find the address of the cell you're currently working on. To move to a different cell, enter the address of that cell in the Name Box and hit Enter. This allows you to navigate within your spreadsheet quickly and efficiently.

3.5.2 Active Cell

The active cell refers to the cell that is currently being referenced. It is the cell that you recently clicked on or moved to. You can easily identify the active cell as it is highlighted on the screen.

3.5.3 Formula Bar

The formula bar displays the contents of the currently selected cell. If the cell contains a formula, the formula is shown in the Formula Bar, while the result of the formula is displayed in the cell itself. To access a dialog box that assists in selecting the correct function and its arguments for the formula, you can click on the fx symbol positioned to the left of the Formula Bar. This feature is optional but can be helpful.

3.6 Scroll Bars

3.6.1 Horizontal or Vertical Split Controls

In Excel, there are handy controls called Horizontal and Vertical Split Controls that allow you to split your worksheet for better viewing. The vertical split control, a small rectangular box situated above the vertical scroll bar, is responsible for dividing the worksheet into two parts. By moving the control downward, you can simultaneously view two different sections of the worksheet. To revert to a single view, simply move the control back to its original position.

Similarly, the horizontal split control that can be found on the right side of the horizontal scroll bar performs an identical function. By moving the control to the left, you can split the worksheet horizontally into two sections for easier navigation and comparison.

3.7 Bottom-Side Components

3.7.1 Worksheet Tabs

A workbook's worksheet tabs are a convenient way to navigate through all the worksheets within a workbook. Initially labeled as Sheet1, Sheet2, and so on, these tabs allow you to effortlessly switch between different worksheets. For easy navigation, you can utilize the small arrow icons located to the left of the worksheet tabs. The first arrow takes you to the first worksheet, the second to the previous one, the third to the next, and the fourth to the last.

To personalize the worksheet names, simply double-click on a tab and enter a new name. Adding a new worksheet is as simple as clicking on the rightmost icon, the New Worksheet Tab Icon. Moreover, you can rearrange the order of the worksheets by left-clicking on a tab and dragging it to a new position in the list. For further options, right-click on any worksheet tab or the tab arrows.

3.7.2 Status Bar

The status bar is a section in the software interface that provides important information to the user. By default, it displays the average, count, and sum values of any selected range. It also includes the zoom in and zoom out sliders, which allow users to adjust the size of the worksheet display. If desired, the information displayed on the status bar can be customized. To do this, simply right-click on the status bar, and a customization dialog box will appear.

Chapter 4: Formulas

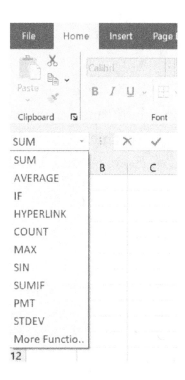

4.1 A Comprehensive Look at Excel Formulas

Excel is a versatile tool that empowers users to collect, process, and analyze data effectively. Among its many features, formulas play a crucial role in harnessing the full potential of Excel.

Formulas in Excel enable users to perform calculations, analyze data, and obtain accurate results swiftly. Their true power becomes evident when handling extensive data sets. By employing the right formula, Excel effortlessly processes massive amounts of information within seconds.

Whether you're a beginner or an experienced user, understanding and utilizing formulas is essential for unlocking Excel's capabilities. In this section, we'll delve into the world of Excel formulas, explore their functionalities, and introduce you to some commonly used built-in functions.

4.1.1 Defining an Excel Formula

In Excel, a formula is an expression that manipulates values in a range of cells. It allows you to perform calculations and analyze data within your spreadsheet. From simple tasks like adding numbers to complex operations like calculating kurtosis, formulas help convert raw data into valuable insights for making informed business decisions.

4.1.2 Defining an Excel Function

On the other hand, a function in Excel is a pre-built formula that provides a shortcut for specific calculations or operations on cell data. With almost 500 functions available and more being added regularly, Excel offers a wide range of tools. However, for most business users, a handful of functions are sufficient to accomplish their tasks effectively.

4.2 How to Create Formulas That Use Data from Other Cells

To create a formula referring to data or values in other cells, follow these steps:

- Choose a cell where you want the formula to be.
- Start the formula by typing the equal sign =.
- Note: In Excel, all formulas begin with an equal sign.
- Select the cell containing the value you want to refer to, or directly type the cell's address.
- Use an operator such as - for subtraction, + for addition, * for multiplication, or / for division.
- Select the next cell you want to include in the formula, or type its address.
- Hit the Enter key on your keyboard. The calculated result will be displayed in the cell with the formula.

4.3 Entering a Formula that Includes a Pre-Set Function

To input a formula with a pre-existing function:

- Choose an empty cell and click on it.
- Begin by typing an equal sign (=) followed by the desired function, like =SUM to calculate total sales.
- Include an opening parenthesis (.
- Select the range of cells and close with a closing parenthesis).
- Press Enter to obtain the final outcome.

4.4 Viewing a Formula

To view a formula, simply enter it into a cell. Once entered, the formula will also be displayed in the formula bar.

- To access the formula bar, all you need to do is select the cell containing the formula.

This allows you to easily see and review the formula you have entered.

4.5 Simple Mathematical Functions and Formulas in Excel

Let's gather these formulas into a collective group, as they are uncomplicated and share a common structure. In Excel, every formula commences with an equal sign (=) and progresses accordingly.

4.5.1 Addition, Subtraction, Multiplication, and Division

- To combine the numbers in two cells, start by clicking on the cell where you want the total to show up.
- Then, type the equal sign (=) to begin the formula.
- Next, click on the cell that contains the first number you want to add. Its cell reference (like D3) will appear alongside the equal sign in the formula.
- Type a plus sign (+) after the first cell reference.
- Then, click on the cell that contains the second number you want to add. Its cell reference (like D4) will appear next to the plus sign. The complete formula to add the values in cells D3 and D4 would be: =D3+D4.

Note:

- Remember that the formula will also be visible in the formula bar above the worksheet. After entering the equal sign in the target cell, you can type the formula in the formula bar. Sometimes, it's easier to work with the entire formula in the formula bar rather than in the worksheet.

- For division, multiplication, and subtraction calculations, the process is similar. Just change the operator (the symbol that indicates the mathematical operation) to a forward slash (/) for division, an asterisk (*) for multiplication, or a minus sign (-) for subtraction.

4.5.2 Using the SUM function to Add Numbers

Adding a group of numbers can be done more quickly. The SUM function that Excel has built-in can help with this.

- To start, click the desired cell where the total should show up.
- Next, to begin the function, type =SUM.
- A drop-down list of choices will appear. To begin, select SUM as an option. =SUM(will now appear in the target cell. A tooltip detailing the SUM syntax can be found directly beneath the cell containing the SUM function. You will see something like this: =SUM([number1, [number2,]...)
- To combine multiple cells, click to select one, enter a comma, click a different cell, and so on. (Or, you

could type another cell reference, a comma, a cell reference, and so on.)

- To add cells one after the other (in a row or column, for example), click the first cell, then press and hold the Shift key to select the last cell in the group. (Or, you can enter the cell references for the first and last cells, separated by a colon; for example, D2:D7 selects D2, D7, along with every cell in between.)
- Press Enter after selecting every cell you'd like to add together.
- The total of the numbers you selected ought to be visible to you as the final result. The entire formula will appear in the formula bar if you highlight the targeted cell once again. In our case, this is =SUM(D2:D7).

It's crucial to remember that every single Excel formula yields relative values. This essentially implies that the final figure will adjust to reflect any changes made to any of the values in the cells that were selected.

To set it as an absolute value—a value that remains constant irrespective of changes made to the cells you used to calculate—you must right-click the cell and click on Copy from the menu that appears. Next, perform another right-click on the cell and choose the Values button (the clipboard icon with 123) under Paste Options.

You will now only see the numeric value in the formula bar when you choose that cell, not a formula.

Excel offers a SUM shortcut under specific conditions. Excel makes the assumption that you intend to add the numbers to a column or row. Excel will automatically select the numbers in a row and add them when you hit Enter if you set your cursor in the cell to the right of the row and click the AutoSum (Σ) button toward the end on the right of the Ribbon's Home tab. Similarly, Excel adds up the values in a column if you point your cursor in the cell beneath a column of numbers, select AutoSum, and press Enter.

4.5.3 Using the AVERAGE Function to Calculate the Average

When you need to find the average of a set of numbers in Excel, you can follow a process similar to the one above. Instead of using the SUM function, you'll use the AVERAGE function. Simply select the cells that contain the numbers you want to include in the calculation and type "=AVERAGE" followed by the selected cells.

Here's a handy tip: if you have a series of numbers in a row or a column, you can use a shortcut to quickly calculate the average. Just place your cursor in the cell to the right of a row of numbers or in the cell below a column of numbers. Click the down arrow next to the AutoSum button, choose Average from the menu, and press Enter. Excel will automatically calculate the average for you.

4.6 The IF Function

This function applies if-then logic to your data to help you streamline the process of making decisions. With the application of this function, you may direct Excel to calculate or show a specific value as a response to a logical test's result. For instance, you could write a test that determines whether a cell's value is more than or equal to 24, in which case it would input "Yes" or "No."

We'll explore using the Formulas tab on the Ribbon, which is an alternative method of entering functions in Excel, while we're learning this particular one. This part has buttons that offer instant access to various functions categorized by name, such as Date & Time, Text, Logical, Financial, AutoSum, and so on. If you are unsure of how to spell a function or can't recall its exact name, it can be useful to be able to browse through them by category.

To input the IF function,

Option #1

- Click the target cell to select it.
- Select the Logical button on the Formulas tab.
- Click on the IF function from the list of functions that is displayed.

Option #2

- A different option is to select the Insert Function button located farthest to the left of the Formulas tab. A list of frequently used functions is displayed in the "Insert Function" pane that opens.
- Click OK after selecting IF from the list. (If the function you've been looking for fails to appear under "Commonly Used," pick another category or All to view all functions that are accessible.)
- You can see =IF() in the target cell when the Function Arguments window opens.

Here is the syntax for the IF function:

=IF(logical_test,"value_if_true","value_if_false")

In the Function Arguments pane of the IF function, you'll find three fields: Logical_test, Value_if_true, and Value_if_false.

Let's consider an example where we want to check if a number in a selected cell is greater than or equal to 24. In this case, the logical test would be E3>=24, the value if true would be "Yes," and the value if false would be "No."

You can input these items in the respective fields of the pane. Alternatively, you can directly enter the complete formula in the desired cell: =IF(E3>=24,"Yes","No"). This formula instructs Excel to display "yes" if the value in cell E3 is greater than or equal to 24, and "no" if it is less than 24.

Remember this handy tip: Instead of manually entering the same function for every row, save time by using the drag-and-drop feature in Excel. Just click and drag the small square in the bottom right corner of the cell with the function. This will automatically fill in the formula for each row, and Excel will adjust the cell references accordingly. For instance, if you use a formula in cell D3 that refers to cell C3, when you drag it to cell D4, it will automatically update to refer to cell C4.

4.7 The CONCAT Function

The CONCAT function is an essential tool for combining text from multiple cells into a single string. It comes in handy when you have separate columns for first and last names and want to merge them. Additionally, it is useful for completing addresses, URLs, file paths, or reference numbers. To use the CONCAT function, simply follow the syntax:

=CONCAT(text1,text2,text3,...)

Let's take an example where we want to merge the list of first names and last names into a full name separated by a space. To achieve this, we can use the CONCAT function in MS Excel. First, we will select the cell where we want to display the full name, let's say D3. Then, we will type =CON and select CONCAT from the drop-down list. After that, we will select the cell containing the first name, for example (B3), add a comma, a blank space enclosed in quotes, and another comma. Following that, we will add the last name by selecting the adjacent cell, say (C3), and pressing Enter. This will give us the formula:

=CONCAT(B3," ",C3)

Finally, we will drag and drop the formula in cell D3 to apply it to all other rows. This will save us the time and effort of manually entering the formula in each cell.

4.8 The SUMIF and COUNTIF Functions

The SUMIF function is an enhanced version of the SUM function, enabling you to calculate the sum of specific values within a range based on your specified criteria. To utilize this function, you need to indicate the range of cells to apply the criteria, define the inclusion criteria, and optionally specify a sum range if it differs from the initial range. The syntax for the SUMIF function is as follows:

=SUMIF(range, criteria, [sum_range])

Please bear in mind that any criteria involving logical operators, mathematical symbols, or text must be enclosed in double quotation marks.

Consider a scenario where you need to calculate the total of sales exceeding $50. The range to evaluate is D3 to D11, with the condition being "greater than 50." In this case, there's no need to specify a separate range for the sum. Thus, your formula would be:

=SUMIF(D3:D11,">50")

Imagine you need to calculate the total sales specifically for the East region. In order to do this, you will need to provide two sets of information: the criteria range (cells C3 to C11) and the sum range (cells D3 to D11). The formula to achieve this is:

=SUMIF(C3:C11,C3,D3:D11)

It's important to note that you don't have to manually enter "East" as the criteria. Instead, you can either type C3 or click on the cell itself to let Excel search for the corresponding text.

You can use a function called COUNTIF to tally the number of values that meet certain conditions. To use this function, follow this syntax:

=COUNTIF(range, criteria)

For example, if you want to count the total sales in the West region, you need to specify the range of cells to apply the criteria to (C3 to C11) and the criteria itself ("West" or the value in cell C4). The formula will look like this:

=COUNTIF(C3:C11, C4)

Have you ever found yourself in a situation where you need to analyze data based on multiple conditions? For example, let's say you want to calculate the total sales for books in the East region or count the number of sales over $50 in the West region. Well, don't sweat it! Excel has got you covered with its powerful functions called SUMIFS and COUNTIFS. These functions allow you to apply multiple criteria to your data, but they do require a slightly more complex syntax compared to their simpler counterparts, SUMIF and COUNTIF.

Chapter 5: The Building Blocks of Microsoft Excel

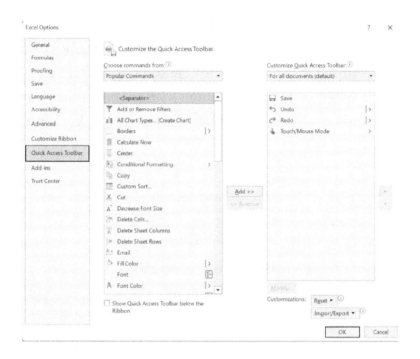

5.1 Customizing the Quick Access Toolbar

In this segment, we will delve into the utilization and personalization of the Quick Access Toolbar in various versions of Excel, including Excel 365, Excel 2021, Excel 2019, Excel 2016, Excel 2013, and Excel 2010. The aim is to simplify accessing frequently used commands. The Quick Access Toolbar serves this purpose perfectly by allowing you to add your preferred commands. With just a click, you can access them effortlessly, regardless of the ribbon tab you are currently browsing.

5.1.1 What is the Quick Access Toolbar?

Located at the very top of the MS Office application window, the Quick Access Toolbar (the QAT) is a tiny, easily customizable toolbar that holds a number of commonly used commands. These commands are accessible from virtually anywhere in the application, regardless of the ribbon tab that is open at the moment.

A preset list of default commands can be accessed using a drop-down menu on the Quick Access Toolbar. These commands can be hidden or shown. It also has a feature where you can add custom commands.

The Quick Access Toolbar has no limit whatsoever on the number of commands it can accept; however, depending on screen size, not every command may be shown.

5.1.2 How to Personalize Excel's Quick Access Toolbar

The Excel Quick Access Toolbar comes preloaded with three buttons: Save, Undo, and Redo. However, if there are additional commands you frequently use, you can easily add them to the toolbar. Customizing the Quick Access

Toolbar in Excel is a simple process, and I'll walk you through it step by step.

To customize the QAT in Microsoft Excel, you can make various adjustments in the Excel Options dialog box. Accessing this option is straightforward, and there are a few ways to do it:

a) Simply right-click on any location on the ribbon and click on "Customize Quick Access Toolbar..." from the menu that appears.
b) Click on the "File" tab, then select "Options," and finally choose "Quick Access Toolbar."
c) Alternatively, click on the small arrow located at the right end of the QAT and select "More Commands" from the menu that pops up.

Whichever method you choose, you'll be directed to the Customize Quick Access Toolbar dialog window. In this window, you have the freedom to rearrange, remove, or add commands in the Quick Access Toolbar to your liking.

5.1.3 Adding a Command Button to the QAT

When it comes to adding a new command, there are three different methods you can use.

5.1.3.1 Adding a Ribbon Button to QAT

The quickest method to include a command from the ribbon in the Quick Access Toolbar is as follows:

- Simply right-click on the command you want from the ribbon.
- From the context menu, choose "Add to Quick Access Toolbar."

That's all there is to it!

5.1.3.2 Using the Predefined List to Enable a Command

To activate a hidden command from the preset list, follow these steps:

- Click the Customize Quick Access Toolbar button and use the downward arrow.
- From the list of commands shown, choose the one you want to activate. That's it!

For instance, if you want to quickly create a new worksheet, proceed to the list, click on the New command, and the related button will instantly appear in the Quick Access Toolbar.

5.1.3.3 Insert a Command in the QAT that Doesn't Appear on the Ribbon

To include a button that isn't visible on the ribbon, follow these steps:

- Right-click on the ribbon and select "Customize Quick Access Toolbar."
- From the drop-down menu that appears on the left, choose "Commands Not in the Ribbon".
- In the commands list located on the left side, select the command you would like to add.
- Click "Add".
- Hit the "OK" button to apply the changes.

5.1.4 Organize Commands in the QAT

To rearrange the sequence of the Quick Access Toolbar commands, follow these steps:

- Launch the Customize the Quick Access Toolbar window.
- On the right-hand area, in the Customize Quick Access Toolbar section, choose the command you wish to reposition, and click either Move Down or Move Up by using the designated arrow.

5.1.5 Removing a Command from the QAT

- To delete a custom or default command from the Quick Access Toolbar, simply right-click on it.
- Choose "Remove from Quick Access Toolbar" from the menu that appears.
- Alternatively, proceed to the Customize the Quick Access Toolbar window and choose the particular command.
- Hit the "Remove" button.

5.1.6 Inserting Macros into the QAT

If you would like to easily access your preferred macros, you can include them in the Quick Access Toolbar (QAT). Follow these steps to do so:

- Launch the Customize the Quick Access Toolbar window.
- In the left drop-down list labeled Choose commands from, pick Macros.

- From the list of macros, choose the one you want to add to the Quick Access Toolbar.
- Hit the Add button.
- Press OK to keep the changes and exit the dialog box.

For instance, let's include a macro that shows every sheet in the current workbook.

You can also choose to insert a separator before the newly added macro.

5.1.7 Grouping Commands on Your QAT

When you have many commands in your Quick Access Toolbar (QAT), it's helpful to organize them into distinct categories. For example, you can separate default commands from custom ones. While the Quick Access Toolbar doesn't have the feature to create groups like the Excel ribbon, you can still group commands by inserting a separator. This can help you locate and use the commands more efficiently.

Here's what you need to do:

- Proceed to the Customize the Quick Access Toolbar dialog window.
- From the list on the left, choose Popular Commands from the drop-down menu.
- Choose <Separator> from the list of commands and click Add.
- Use the Move Up or Move Down arrow to place the separator in the desired position.
- Hit the OK button to save the changes.

5.2 Data Filtering

When you have a lot of stuff on your worksheet, it can be hard to find what you're looking for. Filters help you cut down the data in your worksheet, so you only see what you want to see.

5.2.1 How to Apply Data Filters

Let's say you have a worksheet with a list of equipment, and you want to filter it to show only certain items, like costumes and props. Here's how you can do it:

- Your worksheet should have a header row; this is used to name each column. For instance, the worksheet in our example could have columns A for ID#, Column B for Equipment Type, Column C for Equipment Detail, etc.
- Go to the Data tab and select the Filter command.
- You'll see a drop-down arrow displayed in every column's header cell.
- Select the column you would like to filter by clicking its drop-down arrow. In our case, we'll filter column B to display only specific equipment types.
- A filter menu will pop up.
- Quickly deselect every piece of data by unchecking the box next to Select All.
- Select the checkboxes beside the data you would like to filter, and hit the OK button. For instance, we'll

check costumes and props to display only these equipment types.

- Anything that does not fit the criteria will be immediately hidden as a result of filtering the data. All that will be visible in our case are costumes and props.

More options for filtering can be found via the Sort & Filter command located on the Home tab.

5.2.2 Applying Multiple Filters

When using filters, you can apply more than one to refine your results. For instance, if you've already filtered your worksheet to display costumes and props, you can further refine it to show only costumes and props that were checked out in February by adding another filter.

- To filter a column, click the downward arrow. For instance, to filter column D to display data by date, click its drop-down arrow.
- Then, a filter menu will show up.
- After that, you can select or deselect the boxes based on the data you would like to filter and hit the OK button. As an example, you can deselect all boxes except for February.

- Once you do this, the filter will be applied, and only the costumes and props checked out in February will be displayed in the worksheet.

5.2.3 Clearing Applied Filters

After using a filter, you might like to get rid of it from your sheet so that you can filter the content differently.

- Click the arrow next to the filter you would like to remove. Let's say we want to remove the filter in the column for "Equipment Type."
- A menu will pop up.
- Select "Clear Filter From [NAME of COLUMN]" from the menu. In our case, we'll choose "Clear Filter from 'Equipment Type'."
- The filter will be removed from the column, and the data that was previously hidden will reappear.

5.2.4 Clearing All Filters

- If you would like to remove every filter from your worksheet, go to the Data tab.
- Click on the filter command.

5.2.5 Advanced Filtering

When you're looking for a more specific filter, basic filtering might not offer you all the options you need. Luckily, Excel has various advanced filtering tools, such as number, date, text, and search filtering. These tools can help narrow down your results, making it easier to find exactly what you're looking for.

5.2.5.1 Filtering with Search

In Excel, you can easily search for specific data, such as dates, numbers, or phrases.

- Go to the Data tab and select the Filter command. This will create a drop-down arrow in the header cell for every column. (If your worksheet already has filters added, you can omit this step altogether.)
- Once the filter is enabled, select the drop-down arrow in the header cell of the column containing the data you would like to filter.
- You will see a filter menu. Simply type your search term in the provided search box, and the results will automatically show up below.
- Hit the OK when you're done.

Your worksheet will then be filtered based on your search term.

5.2.5.2 Advanced Number Filters

Advanced number filters let you manage numerical data in various ways. For instance, you can choose to show specific types of equipment by setting a range of ID numbers.

- To filter data in Excel, proceed to the Ribbon, click on the Data tab, and select Filter. This will add a drop-down arrow in the header cell for every column. If your worksheet already has filters added, you can proceed to the next step.
- Next, click the drop-down arrow beside the column you would like to filter. For instance, if you would like to filter column A to display a specific range of ID numbers,
- Then, you will see the Filter menu. Place your mouse over the number filters and click on the filter you like from the drop-down list. For instance, you can pick Between to display ID numbers within a specific range.
- After that, you will see a Custom AutoFilter dialog box. Proceed to the right side of every filter, type in the specific numbers, and hit the OK button. For instance, if you would like to filter for ID numbers

between 4000 and 8000, enter these values and hit the OK button.

- Once done, your data will be filtered according to the number filter that you selected. In this case, only items with an ID number between 4000 and 8000 will be displayed.

5.2.5.3 Advanced Text Filters

You can use advanced text filters to show precise data, such as cells with a specific character count or data that does not include a certain number or word. For instance, we can exclude any item that includes the word "costume."

- Navigate to the Data tab and select the Filter command. This action will cause a drop-down arrow to appear in every column's header cell. Please bear in mind that if filters are already in place, you can proceed to the next step.
- Select the drop-down arrow for the specific column you would like to filter.
- You will see a filter menu. Hover your mouse over the text filters and choose the desired text filter from the listed options. For instance, choosing "Does Not Contain..." allows you to see data that doesn't include specific text.
- You will see a pop-up dialog box labeled "Custom AutoFilter." Move to the right of the filter, type the

desired text, and then select OK. For instance, entering "costume" will exclude any items containing this word.

- The data will then be filtered according to the selected text filter. In our chosen example, the worksheet will show only items that do not contain the word "costume."

5.2.5.4 Advanced Date Filters

You can use advanced date filters to see data from specific time frames, like the previous year, upcoming quarter, or within two dates. For instance, we can apply advanced date filters to display equipment that was checked out between May 10 and October 10.

- Select the Filter command in the Data tab. This will display a drop-down arrow in every column's header cell.
- Proceed to the column you would like to filter and select its drop-down arrow.
- You will see a filter menu. Place your cursor over Date Filters and click on the specific date filter from the displayed drop-down menu, such as Between..., to display specific dates.
- Enter the dates you want to filter in the dialog box labeled "Custom AutoFilter" and hit OK to apply the filter.

The worksheet will now display the filtered data based on your selected date range.

5.3 Adding Dynamic Headers and Footers

When using Excel, you can find different ready-made choices to help you make flexible headers and footers for your worksheets. You can access these choices through the Page Layout tab in the Excel ribbon.

- To include a pre-made header or footer, simply select the Insert Header or Insert Footer button.
- You have the flexibility to select from different choices, including showing the sheet name, page number, or file path in the header or footer.
- Excel also allows you to insert the time, date, or your own text into the header or footer.

5.3.1 Adding File Names, Page Numbers, Dates, and Other Dynamic Components

In Excel, dynamic elements such as file names, page numbers, and dates can update automatically, eliminating the need for manual updates each time the worksheet is saved or printed.

- To include page numbers, click the Page Number button in the Design tab and select your desired format. Excel will automatically add the correct page number to each printed page.

- Likewise, to insert the current date into the header or footer, navigate to the Design tab while editing the header or footer, then select the Date button. Choose the date format you prefer, and Excel will add the current date for you.
- If you wish to add the file name to the header or footer, proceed to the Design tab and select the File Path button. Excel will then fill in the header or footer with the full path or name of the currently open file.

5.3.2 Using Special Characters, Images, and Text to Personalize Headers and Footers

Although the default choices are a good place to start, you may find yourself needing to further adjust the headers and footers to fit your exact needs.

- Begin by double-clicking on the header or footer section to input personalized text. Input text, and use the formatting options on the Excel toolbar to style the text as desired.
- To add images to the header or footer, navigate to the Insert tab and select the Picture button. Choose the image to be inserted and modify its size and placement within the header or footer.
- Access special characters, like trademark or copyright symbols, through the Symbol button in the Insert tab. Simply select your preferred symbol

and hit the Insert option to add it to the header or footer.

5.4 Defining or Clearing a Print Area on Your Worksheet

If you often need to print a particular part of a worksheet, you can set a print area to include only that part. A print area is a range of cells that you select for printing when you don't want to print the whole worksheet. Once you've set a print area, only that specific part will be printed when you print the worksheet. You can also add more cells to the print area as you need, and you can remove the print area to print the entire worksheet.

It's possible for a worksheet to have multiple print areas, and each print area will be printed on a separate page.

5.4.1 Creating One or Multiple Print Areas

To create one or multiple print areas in Excel, follow these steps:

- Select the cells on your worksheet that you would like to define as a print area. If you would like to create more than one print area, hold down the Ctrl key and select the areas you would like to print. Every print area will be printed on a separate page.

- Proceed to the Page Layout tab, then in the Page Setup group, select the Print Area and choose Set Print Area.

After your workbook has been saved, the print area that you specified will be retained.

Proceed to View, navigate to the Workbook Views group, and click on Page Break Preview to view all the print areas and confirm they are as you would like. The print area is stored along with your workbook when you save it.

5.4.2 Adding Cells to an Already-Existing Print Area

To increase the print area in Excel, you can simply add cells that are next to the existing print area. When you add cells that are not next to the print area, Excel makes a new print area for those cells.

- Choose the cells you wish to include in the print area of the worksheet. If the cells are not next to the existing print area, a new print area will be created, and each print area will be printed on a different page. Only cells adjacent to the existing print area can be added.

- Go to the Page Layout tab and select the Print Area in the Page Setup group. Then select Add to Print Area.
- Remember, the print area is stored along with your workbook when you save it.

5.4.3 Removing a Print Area

If your worksheet has more than one print area, getting rid of one will get rid of them all. Here's how to do it:

- Click on the worksheet that has the print area you want to clear.
- Proceed to the Page Layout tab, go to the Page Setup group, and hit Clear Print Area.

5.5 Hiding Detailed Data by Grouping or Ungrouping Columns

When dealing with a large number of columns in your Excel worksheet, it can be helpful to group them for easier organization. This allows you to hide or unhide different sections of the sheet with ease. To group columns in Excel, follow these steps:

5.5.1 Grouping Columns

- To group columns in Excel, start by selecting every column you would like to group, or just a cell for every column.
- Then, go to the Data tab and select Group in the Outline group, or push the Shift + Alt + Right Arrow keys at once.
- If you haven't selected complete columns, a dialog box will appear, prompting you to choose columns or rows. Select columns and hit the OK button.

5.5.2 Hiding/Unhiding Columns

- Proceed to the top of the group to select the minus "-" sign if you intend to conceal the columns.
- You can also expand and collapse groups by making use of the outline numbers in the top-left area.
- Click the minus "-" sign to reveal the columns.

5.5.3 Clear Grouping

To clear column grouping, follow these steps:

5.5.3.1 Ungrouping Specific Columns

- If you want to ungroup specific columns, choose those columns.

- Proceed to the Data tab. Hit the Ungroup button or use the Shift + Alt + Left Arrow shortcut.

5.5.3.2 Ungrouping All Columns

If you would like to ungroup every column at any existing level, navigate to the Data tab.

- Click on the Outline group.
- Select the arrow under Ungroup before selecting Clear Outline.

5.6 Financial Models: Tracing Dependents and Precedents

Understanding the connections between formulas and variables is vital in financial modeling. Trace dependents and trace precedents are tools that help in financial analysis to swiftly pinpoint errors and ensure all outputs and inputs are correctly linked. This is particularly crucial in complex financial models with many calculations and variables, where even a small mistake can greatly affect the final results.

5.6.1 Excel Trace Dependents

In Excel, the Trace Dependents tool helps you identify which cells are impacted by the value of a specific cell. Follow these steps:

- Choose the cell you would like to trace dependents for.
- Navigate to the "Formulas" tab and locate the "Formula Auditing" group.
- Select the "Trace Dependents" option (or use Ctrl +]). Excel will display arrows indicating the cells affected by the value of the cell that was selected.
- If the cell has more than one dependent, you can trace the dependents of the dependent cells by using the "Trace Dependents" button once again.
- Proceed to the "Formula Auditing" group and select the "Remove Arrows" option to get rid of the arrows.

5.6.2 Excel Trace Precedents

To uncover the cells involved in calculating one selected cell in Microsoft Excel, use the Trace Precedents tool:

- Choose the cell you would like to trace precedents for.

- Navigate to the "Formulas" tab and locate the "Formula Auditing" group.
- Select the "Trace Precedents" option (or use Ctrl +]). Excel will then display arrows to indicate the cells involved in the calculation of the cell that was selected.
- If the cell has more than one precedent, you can trace the precedents of the precedent cells by using the "Trace Precedents" button once again.
- Proceed to the "Formula Auditing" group and select the "Remove Arrows" option to get rid of the arrows.

5.7 Application of Data Validation in Cells

When working with spreadsheets, you can use data validation to control the value or data types that users can input into a cell, such as when creating a drop-down list. Here's how to use data validation in Excel:

- Choose the cell or cells for which you would like to set up the validation rule.
- Go to the Data tab and select Data Validation.
- Under Allow in the Settings tab, choose an option like Custom, Text length, Time, Date, List, Decimal, or Whole Number.
- Choose a condition under Data.

- Enter the necessary values depending on your choices for Allow and Data.
- Personalize a message for users on the Input Message tab.
- Check the box to show the input message when the user hovers over or selects the cell or cells.
- Personalize the error message and select a style on the Error Alert tab.
- Click OK to apply the data validation.

By setting up data validation, you can ensure that users input only valid values, and if they try to input something invalid, an error message will appear with your personalized text.

Chapter 6: A Quick Excel Journey with Shortcuts

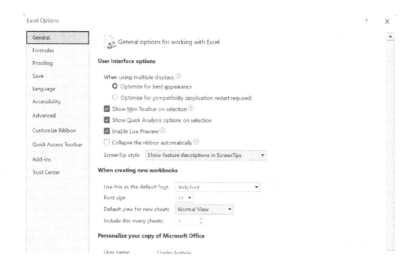

6.1 Keyboard Shortcuts

- To select all, press Ctrl+A.
- To make text bold, use Ctrl+B.
- To copy, press Ctrl+C.
- For a fill-down, press Ctrl+D.
- To use Flash Fill, press Ctrl+E.
- To find, press Ctrl+F.
- To go to a specific location, use Ctrl+G.
- To replace, press Ctrl+H.
- To italicize text, use Ctrl+I.
- For inserting a hyperlink, press Ctrl+K.
- To create a new workbook, press Ctrl+N.

- To open a file, press Ctrl+O.
- For printing, press Ctrl+P.
- To fill to the right, press Ctrl+R.
- To save, press Ctrl+S.
- To underline text, use Ctrl+U.
- For pasting, press Ctrl+V.
- To close, press Ctrl+W.
- To cut, use Ctrl+X.
- For a redo, press Ctrl+Y.
- To undo, use Ctrl+Z.
- To get help, press F1.
- For editing, use F2.
- If you would like to paste a name, use the F3 key.
- For repeating the last action, press F4.
- When switching between relative and absolute references while typing a formula, use F4.
- To go to a specific location, press the F5 key.
- For moving to the next pan, use F6.
- To check your spelling, press F7.
- To extend mode, press the F8 key.
- For recalculating every workbook, use F9.
- To activate the menu bar, press F10.
- To create a new chart, use the F11 key.
- If you want to save as a file, hit the F12 key.
- For inserting the current time, use Ctrl+:
- For inserting the current date, use Ctrl+;
- If you would like to copy the value of the cell above, press Ctrl+"

- For copying the formula in the cell above, use Ctrl+'
- For other functions in MS Excel's menu, press and hold down the Shift key.
- Press Shift+F1 for help.
- To edit a cell comment, use Shift+F2.
- If you want to paste a function into a formula, press Shift+F3.
- Press Shift+F4 to find the next occurrence of a term.
- Use Shift+F5 to find something in your document.
- To switch to the previous pane, press Shift+F6.
- Press Shift+F8 to add to your selection.
- If you want to recalculate the active worksheet, press Shift+F9.
- Press Ctrl+Alt+F9 to recalculate every worksheet in your open workbooks, even if there haven't been any changes.
- If you want to double-check all the formulas that rely on other cells and then calculate every cell in your open workbooks, which includes the ones that weren't flagged for calculation, use Ctrl+Alt+Shift+F9.
- To bring up a shortcut menu, hit Shift+F10.
- Create a new worksheet by pressing Shift+F11.
- Save your work by pressing Shift+F12.
- Define a name for a specific cell or range of cells by using Ctrl+F3.
- Close the current workbook with Ctrl+F4.
- Restore the size of the Excel window with Ctrl+F5.

- Move to the next workbook window with Ctrl+F6.
- To move to the previous workbook window, press Shift+Ctrl+F6.
- Move the current workbook window with Ctrl+F7.
- Resize the current workbook window with Ctrl+F8.
- Minimize the current workbook with Ctrl+F9.
- Restore or maximize the window size with Ctrl+F10.
- For the Inset 4.0 macro sheet, use Ctrl+F11.
- Open a file with Ctrl+F12.
- For inserting a chart, press Alt+F1.
- Save your file with a different name using Alt+F2.
- Exit Excel with Alt+F4.
- Access the macro dialog box with Alt+F8.
- Open the Visual Basic Editor with Alt+F11.
- To create a name by using column and row labels, press Ctrl+Shift+F3.
- Use Ctrl+Shift+F6 to go to the previous window.
- Press Ctrl+Shift+F12 to print.
- To start a new worksheet, press Alt+Shift+F1.
- To save, use Alt+Shift+F2.
- For AutoSum, press Alt+=.
- Toggle between formula and value display with Ctrl+`.
- Insert argument names into a formula using Ctrl+Shift+A.
- Use the Alt+Down arrow to make the AutoComplete list visible.
- Press Alt+' for the Format Style dialog box.

- To apply specific formats, use the following shortcuts:
a) Ctrl+Shift+~ for general,
b) Ctrl+Shift+! for a comma,
c) Ctrl+Shift+@ for time,
d) Ctrl+Shift+# for date,
e) Ctrl+Shift+$ for currency,
f) Ctrl+Shift+% for percent, and
g) Ctrl+Shift+^ for exponential.

- Use Ctrl+Shift+& to place an outline border around selected cells.
- Press Ctrl+Shift+_ to get rid of the outline border.
- To select the current region around the active cell or the full PivotTable report in a PivotTable report, press Ctrl+Shift+*.
- Depending on the selection, use Ctrl++ to insert cells, columns, or rows.
- Use Ctrl+- to delete any inserted cells, columns, or rows.
- Access the Format Cells dialog box with Ctrl+1.
- Apply text formatting with Ctrl+2 for bold.
- Ctrl+3 for italic,
- Ctrl+4 for underline, and
- Ctrl+5 for strikethrough.
- To display or conceal objects, use Ctrl+6.
- To display or conceal the standard toolbar, press Ctrl+7.
- Toggle outline symbols with Ctrl+8.

- Hide rows with Ctrl+9.
- Hide columns with Ctrl+0.
- To unhide rows, press Ctrl+Shift+(.
- To unhide columns, use Ctrl+Shift+).
- To activate the menu, press Alt or F10.
- Navigate between toolbars or workbooks with Ctrl+Tab and Shift+Ctrl+Tab, respectively.
- To move to the next tool, use Tab.
- To go to the previous tool, press Shift+Tab.
- For executing a command, press Enter.
- To begin a new line in the same cell, use Alt+Enter.
- To populate your chosen cell range with the current entry, use Ctrl+Enter.
- If you would like to access the font drop-down list, press Shift+Ctrl+F.
- To launch the format cell dialog box's Font tab, use Shift+Ctrl+F+F.
- To choose the point size from the drop-down list, press Shift+Ctrl+P.
- If you would like to select the whole column, hit Ctrl+Spacebar.
- For selecting the whole row, use Shift+Spacebar.
- Return to the active cell, bringing it into view, and use CTRL+Backspace.
- For Selecting the array that contains the active cell, press CTRL+/.
- Choose every cell containing comments; use CTRL+SHIFT+O.

- For selecting cells that do not match the static value or formula in an active cell in a selected row, use CTRL+\.
- For selecting cells that do not match the static value or formula in an active cell in a selected column, press CTRL+SHIFT+|.
- For selecting cells directly or indirectly referenced by formulas in the selection, use CTRL+[and CTRL+SHIFT+{.
- For selecting cells containing formulas that directly or indirectly reference the active cell, press CTRL+] and CTRL+SHIFT+}.
- To choose the visible cells in the active selection, use ALT+;.
- For selecting the active cell, when multiple cells are selected, use SHIFT+BACKSPACE.
- To select the whole worksheet, press the CTRL+SHIFT+SPACEBAR keys.
- For reapplying the filter and sort feature on the selected range to include changes made, use Ctrl+Alt+L.
- To make the Paste Special dialog box visible after cutting or copying content, press Ctrl+Alt+V.

Chapter 7: Advanced Uses of Excel

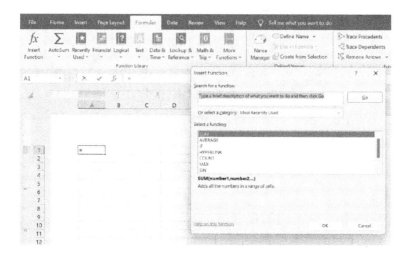

7.1 Working with Advanced Formulas and Functions

Microsoft Excel contains a set of advanced formulas that are not frequently utilized. These built-in formulas enable users to extract specific data from an existing dataset, such as by filtering based on specific criteria, duplicating data, or applying conditional formulas. These functions are instrumental in creating dashboards, generating reports, and performing other complex data manipulation tasks within Excel.

In this section, we'll explore some of the most advanced functions and formulas in Excel. They are as follows:

7.2 The INDEX Formula

The INDEX formula in Excel is a powerful function that allows users to retrieve data from a specific row and column within a given array. Its syntax is straightforward, consisting of the array from which to retrieve the data, the row number, and the column number. Here's a simple example:

=INDEX(A1:D10, 3, 2)

In this example, A1:D10 is the array, 3 represents the row number, and 2 represents the column number. This formula would return the value at the intersection of the third row and second column within the specified array.

7.3 The VLOOKUP Formula

The VLOOKUP formula is widely used in Excel because of its simplicity and its ability to find a specific value in other tables based on a common variable. For instance, if we have two tables with employee names and salaries and we want to find the salary from Table B in Table A using "Employee ID" as the common variable, we can use VLOOKUP. Its syntax is straightforward:

=VLOOKUP(lookup_value, table_array, col_index_num, [range_lookup]).

Applying this formula to the "Employee Salary" column will populate the table with the desired data when the formula is dragged to other cells.

7.4 The IF AND Formula

The IF AND formula in Excel allow you to test multiple conditions at the same time. Its syntax is "=IF(AND(condition1, condition2), value_if_true, value_if_false)."

Here's a simple example: =IF(AND(A2>10, B2="Yes"), "Good", "Bad").

This formula checks if cell A2 is greater than 10 and cell B2 contains "yes." If both conditions are met, it returns "good"; otherwise, it returns "bad."

7.5 The MATCH Formula

The MATCH formula in Excel is a handy function that helps you locate the position of a specific item within a range. Its syntax is straightforward:

=MATCH(lookup_value, lookup_array, [match_type]).
Here, lookup_value is the value you want to find,
lookup_array is the range of cells to search, and
match_type (optional) specifies the type of match.

For example, =MATCH(5, A1:A10, 0) would return the
position of the value 5 in the range A1:A10, using the exact
match (0). This can be especially useful in large datasets for
quickly finding relevant information.

7.6 The SUMIF Formula

The SUMIF formula in Excel is a powerful tool for adding
up values that meet specific criteria. Its syntax is
straightforward: =SUMIF(range, criteria, sum_range).

Here's a simple example: Let's say you have a list of sales
figures in column A and corresponding salespeople's names
in column B. To sum the sales figures for a specific
salesperson, you can use the formula =SUMIF(B2:B10,
"John", A2:A10). This will add up all the sales figures for
the salesperson named "John."

7.7 The IF OR Formula

The IF OR formula in Excel allows you to test multiple
conditions at the same time. Its syntax is straightforward:

=IF(OR(condition1, condition2), value_if_true, value_if_false).

Here's a simple example: Let's say you want to check if either A1 or B1 contains the word "apple," and if so, return "yes." The formula would look like this: =IF(OR(A1="apple", B1="apple"), "Yes", "No"). This formula checks both A1 and B1 for the presence of "apple" and returns "yes" if either contains it, otherwise "no."

7.8 The LEFT, MID, and RIGHT Formulas

The LEFT, MID, and RIGHT formulas are used to extract specific parts of a text string.

Left: This formula returns a specific number of characters from the start of a text string. Its syntax is =LEFT(text, num_chars). For example, =LEFT("Excel is awesome", 5) would return "Excel".

Mid: The MID formula extracts a specific number of characters from the middle of a text string. Its syntax is =MID(text, start_num, num_chars). For instance, =MID("Excel is awesome", 7, 2) would return "is".

Right: This formula returns a specific number of characters from the end of a text string. Its syntax is =RIGHT(text, num_chars). For example, =RIGHT("Excel is awesome", 6) would return "awesome".

These formulas are handy for manipulating and extracting specific parts of text within Excel spreadsheets.

7.9 The CONCATENATE Formula

The CONCATENATE formula in Excel combines multiple strings into one. Its syntax is straightforward: =CONCATENATE(text1, [text2],...).

For instance, to join "Hello" and "World" into "Hello World," use =CONCATENATE("Hello", "", "World"). This formula is handy for merging text from different cells or adding spaces between words.

It's a useful tool for creating personalized messages, generating dynamic report titles, or any situation where you need to combine text in Excel.

7.10 The TRIM Formula

The TRIM function in Excel removes extra spaces from a string of text, leaving only single spaces between words. Its syntax is straightforward: =TRIM(text).

For instance, if you have a cell containing " Hello World " and you want to remove the excess spaces, you can use =TRIM(A1) to get "Hello World." This can be quite handy when working with data imported from other sources, ensuring that everything looks neat and tidy without the hassle of manually editing each cell.

7.11 The Offset Formula

The OFFSET formula in Excel is a powerful function that allows you to reference a range of cells and return a new range that is a specified number of rows and columns away from the original range. Its syntax is =OFFSET(reference, rows, cols, [height], [width]).

For example, if you have data in cells A1:A5 and you want to reference a range of cells that starts 2 rows below and 1 column to the right of A1, you can use the formula =OFFSET(A1,2,1,1,1). This will return the value in cell B3.

This formula is useful for dynamic data analysis and manipulation in Excel.

7.12 Key Points to Remember

- Ensure to enter the right function names to avoid receiving the "#NAME?" error.
- Check for empty cells before using formulas to prevent "#VALUE!" or "#NA" errors.
- Use the correct cell values (alpha-numeric or numeric) to avoid the "#NUM!" error when entering cell references or argument values.

Chapter 8: MS Excel Tables

In this section, we'll cover the basics of the table format, demonstrating how to create a table in Microsoft Excel and make the most of its robust capabilities.

At first glance, an Excel table might seem like a simple tool for arranging data. However, this seemingly basic feature actually encompasses a wide range of useful functions. Excel tables can effortlessly recalculate and sum up thousands of columns and rows, as well as sort, filter, update, reformat, summarize with pivot tables, and export data.

8.1 What is an Excel Table?

You might think your worksheet data is in a table because it's organized in columns and rows. But it's not a real "table" unless you've designated it as one.

An Excel table is a unique object that functions as a whole. It lets you control the table's contents separately from the rest of the worksheet data.

Excel tables offer a wealth of powerful features beyond just a collection of organized data and headers.

- Supports the integration of filter and sort options, along with visual filtering using slicers.
- They dynamically expand and contract as you add or remove columns and rows.
- Column headings continue to be visible while you scroll to improve usability.
- Simplified formatting using built-in table styles.
- Calculated columns enable the computation of whole columns when you type a formula in a cell.
- Quick totals for summing, counting, averaging, and finding min or max values with a single click.
- As data is added or removed from the table, dynamic charts update seamlessly.
- Formulas are readable, using a distinct syntax that utilizes table and column names instead of cell references.

8.2 Creating Your Own Table in MS Excel

To transform a range of cells into a table in Excel, follow these steps:

- Choose any cell from your dataset.
- Navigate to the Insert tab and click on the Table button in the Tables group, or use the Ctrl + T keys on your keyboard.
- A dialog box will show up, seamlessly selecting your data on your behalf. You can modify the range if necessary. If you would like to turn the first row of data into table headers, ensure the "My table has headers" option is checked.
- Select Ok to apply changes.

By doing this, the application will convert your data range into a proper table that comes in the default style.

8.3 Quick Tips and Recommendations

- When you insert a table, Microsoft Excel keeps all the formatting you have. To avoid any issues with the table style, it's a good idea to remove some existing formatting, like background colors.
- Before making a table, tidy up your data first. Remove any empty rows, give every column a clear

name, and ensure that every row has information about one thing.

- You can have more than one table on a sheet if you need to. For easier reading, it makes sense to add at least one empty column and one empty row between other data and the table.

8.4 Choosing a Selected Style for Your Table

Creating a table in Excel is quick, but it always uses the default style. If you want to use a specific style, follow these steps:

- Click on any cell within your data to select it.
- Go to the Home tab and select Format as Table in the Styles group.
- Choose the style you would like from the gallery.
- If needed, adjust the range in the Create Table dialog box, check the My table has headers box, and select OK to apply changes.

Quick Tip: You should right-click the style and select Apply and Clear Formatting to apply your chosen style and clear any formatting that was present.

8.5 Giving Your Table a Name

When you create a table in Excel, it's inevitably assigned a default name like Table1, Table2, and so on. If you're working with more than one table, giving them descriptive and clear names can simplify your work significantly.

Renaming a table is a simple process. Follow these steps:

- Click on any cell within the table.
- Navigate to the Table Design tab and locate the Properties group. Then, click on the current name in the Table Name box and replace it with the new name you would like to use.

Quick Tip: Press Ctrl + F3 to open the Name Manager and see a list of all the tables in the current workbook.

8.6 Filtering and Sorting

Excel tables offer a range of useful features beyond basic data manipulation. These features are typically easy to understand and use. Here's a brief look at two of the most significant features:

8.6.1 Sorting Your Excel Table

- To sort an Excel table by a particular column, all you need to do is select the drop-down arrow in the header cell and choose the sorting option you need.

8.6.2 Filtering Your Excel Table

To enable data filtering in a table, follow these steps:

- To begin, select the drop-down arrow in the column header.
- Next, deselect the checkboxes beside the data you would like to remove. Alternatively, deselect the Select All box to clear every selection, and then select the checkboxes beside the data you would like to display.
- If needed, you can utilize the Text Filters and Filter by Color options.
- Finally, select OK to apply the changes.

To remove the arrows from your table if you don't need the auto-filter feature, go to the Design tab and uncheck the Filter Button box in the Table Style Options group. You can also use the Ctrl + Shift + L shortcut to toggle the filter buttons on and off.

If you want to create a visual filter for your table, you can add a slicer by clicking Insert Slicer on the Table Design tab in the Tools group.

8.7 Table Styles

Formatting Excel tables is simple, seeing as you have a range of predefined styles to choose from. You can also customize your own style to match your preferences.

8.7.1 Changing the Style of Your Excel Table

Whenever a table is added in Excel, it automatically gets a default style. If you want to modify the style, follow these steps:

- Click on any cell within the table.
- Go to the Design tab and choose the style you like in the Table Styles group. If you wish to see more styles, select the More button in the bottom right area.

8.7.2 Setting the New Style as Default

To modify the standard table style, simply right-click on the style you prefer and select "Set as Default." This will apply the new default table style to any new tables created within the same workbook.

8.7.3 Clearing Current Formatting While Applying Table Style

In Excel, if you apply a predefined style to a table, the program will retain the current formatting.

- To clear any previous formatting, simply right-click the style and select "Apply and Clear Formatting."

8.7.4 How to Get Rid of a Table's Formatting

To remove formatting from an Excel table while retaining all its functions, follow these steps:

- Click on any cell in the table.
- Navigate to the Design tab, located in the Table Styles group. Select the More button in the lower-right area, and then select Clear under the table-style templates. Alternatively, choose the first style under Light, labeled None.

Please be aware that this approach solely eliminates the pre-existing table formatting while retaining your customized formatting.

- If you wish to erase all formatting within a table entirely, navigate to the Home tab.
- Click on the Formats group.
- Select Clear and click on Clear Formats.

8.8 Removing an Excel Table

To take out a table, simply follow these steps:

- To turn your table into a range, simply right-click any cell within the table, select Table, and click on Convert to Range. Alternatively, you can find the Tools group and use the Convert to Range button located on the Design tab.
- Confirm your action by clicking "Yes" in the dialog box that pops up.

When you clear the table, all formatting and data will be retained. If you would like to keep only the data, you should get rid of the table formatting before you convert the table to a range.

Chapter 9: MS Excel Charts

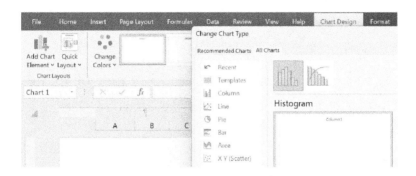

Interpreting large Excel workbooks with extensive data can be challenging. Using charts to visually represent workbook data makes it easier to understand and compare trends.

9.1 Working with Charts

In Excel, there are various chart options to help you present your data effectively. Understanding the different types of charts in Excel is key to using them to their full potential. Here are some of the chart types you can use in Excel:

9.1.1 Surface Charts

Surface charts present data across a three-dimensional landscape, making them ideal for visualizing huge data sets and gaining insights from multiple pieces of information simultaneously.

9.1.2 Area Charts

Area charts resemble line charts, but they fill in the areas under the lines.

9.1.3 Bar Charts

Bar charts function similarly to column charts, except they utilize horizontal bars instead of vertical ones.

9.1.4 Pie Charts

Pie charts simplify comparing proportions. Every value is represented as a pie slice, making it easy to identify the values comprising a percentage of the whole.

9.1.5 Line Charts

Line charts work great for displaying trends. By connecting the data points with lines, it becomes simple to observe if the values are going up or down over time.

9.1.6 Column Charts

Column charts employ vertical bars to depict data. They are versatile and commonly utilized for comparing various types of information.

9.2 Inserting a Chart

- To create a chart in Excel, start by choosing the cells for the chart, which include row labels and column titles. The selected cells will provide the data for the chart.
- Next, go to the Insert tab and select the Chart command.
- Then, select the type of chart you want from the drop-down menu.
- The chosen chart will then be added to your worksheet.

When you're unsure about the chart type to use, you can rely on the Recommended Charts command to propose various charts based on your data.

9.3 Changing Your Chart and Layout Style

Once you've added a chart, you might want to make some adjustments to how your data appears. You can easily modify a chart's layout and design using the options available in the Design tab.

9.3.1 Modifying the Appearance of Your Chart

In Excel, there are various chart styles that let you easily change the appearance of your chart. To modify the chart style, choose the style you would like from the Chart Styles group. You can also proceed to the right and select the drop-down arrow to view additional styles.

9.3.2 Adding Chart Elements, such as Data Labels, Legends, and Chart Titles

In Excel, you can enhance your chart by adding elements such as data labels, legends, and chart titles.

- To do this, proceed to the Design tab and select the Add Chart Element command.
- From there, choose the specific element you want to add from the drop-down menu.

9.3.3 Using Predefined Layouts Instead of Individual Chart Elements

In Excel, you can save time by using predefined layouts for your charts instead of adding elements one by one.

- Just locate the Quick Layout command, click on it, and select the layout you want from the menu.

9.3.4 Editing a Chart Element

- To modify a chart element, such as a chart title, just double-click on the placeholder and start to type.

9.3.5 Chart Formatting Buttons

You may employ the chart formatting shortcut buttons to promptly alter the chart style, incorporate chart elements, and refine chart data.

9.4 Bringing More Customization to Your Charts

Excel offers various options for customizing and arranging your charts. You can modify the type of chart, reorganize its data, and relocate the chart within the workbook.

9.4.1 Switching to a Different Type of Chart

If your data doesn't look right in one type of chart, you can easily try a different type. For example, you can change a bar chart to a pie chart.

- Click on Change Chart Type in the Design tab.
- A box will pop up. Choose a different layout and type of chart.
- Select Ok to apply changes.
- The new chart type will show up.

9.4.2 Switching Column and Row Data

When working with charts, you might find it helpful to rearrange the way data is grouped. For instance, if you have a chart displaying book sales data, the information may be grouped by genre with columns for every month. You could interchange columns and rows if you want the chart to group the data per month with columns that represent every genre. The data on the chart is the same in both instances; it is simply arranged differently.

- Pick the chart you would like to change.
- Click on the Swap Row/Column option on the Design tab.
- The columns and rows will swap places.

9.4.3 Moving a Chart to a Different Worksheet

When you add a new chart, it shows up as an object on the worksheet where the data is. You can move the chart to a different worksheet to keep your data neat and organized.

- Choose the chart you would like to move.
- From the Design tab, locate the Move Chart option and click on it.
- A dialog box will pop up. Pick the location where you would like to move the chart. For instance, you can move your chart to a new worksheet by selecting New Sheet.
- Click OK to apply the changes.
- You will see the chart in its new position.

9.5 Keeping Your Charts Updated

When you input additional data into your spreadsheet, the chart might not automatically update to include the new data. To rectify this, you can modify the data range. Just select the chart, and it will show the data range in your spreadsheet. Then, you can adjust the data range by clicking and dragging the handle located in the bottom-right corner.

If you often add new information to your spreadsheet, it can be a hassle to update the data range. However, there's a simple solution. Just format the original data into a table format, and then generate a chart from that table. More data can be added under the table, and it will immediately be updated and incorporated into both the table and the chart. This keeps everything consistent.

Chapter 10

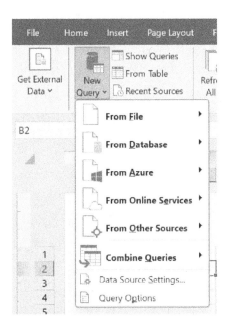

10.1 Defining Data Analysis

Data analysis involves cleaning, transforming, and examining raw data to obtain useful information for making informed business decisions. It provides data and insights in visual formats like graphs, tables, and charts, which help mitigate decision-making risks.

10.2 What is Data Analytics and Visualization?

Data analytics goes beyond just analyzing data. It includes collecting, organizing, storing, and using tools to explore data. It also involves presenting findings through data visualization tools. On the other hand, data analysis focuses on turning raw data into useful information, statistics, and explanations.

10.3 What is Data Visualization?

Data visualization involves presenting data in graphical form. It's especially useful for large datasets, like time series, making it easier to convey information visually.

10.4 Defining Data Mapping

Data mapping shows how the features of these elements shift based on the information. For example, a bar chart represents the size of a variable by the length of a bar. Data visualization relies on mapping, and poorly designed mapping can make it harder to read a chart.

10.5 A Quick Introduction to Data Analysis Using Excel

Analyzing data is an important skill that can improve decision-making. Microsoft Excel stands out as a widely used data analysis tool, and its pivot tables are especially favored for data analysis.

In Microsoft Excel, you can explore and understand data in many ways. The data may come from various sources and be in different formats. Excel offers tools like PowerMap, PowerView, PowerPivot, Data Model, Solvers, What-If Analysis, Inquire Tool, Formula Auditing, Quick Analysis, Subtotals, Financial Functions, Time Functions, Date Functions, Text Functions, Tables, Ranges, Conditional Formatting, and other tools, functions, and commands to help you analyze it.

10.6 Important Functions for Excel Data Analysis

With Excel boasting numerous functions, it can be daunting to pair the right formula with specific data analysis. However, the most valuable functions need not be complex. Discover the following simple functions that will enhance your data interpretation skills, making you wonder how you managed without them.

10.6.1 Len()

When analyzing data, the LEN function is handy for counting the number of characters in each cell. It's commonly used when dealing with text that has a specific character limit or when trying to differentiate between product numbers.

The syntax for using the LEN function is: LEN(text)

10.6.2 Concatenate

When you're analyzing data, the =CONCATENATE formula is super simple yet really potent. It lets you merge text, numbers, dates, and other data from multiple cells into one single cell.

The syntax is: =CONCATENATE (text1, text2, [text3],...)

10.6.3 Networkdays

The "Networkdays" function in Excel automatically excludes weekends when used, making it easier to calculate workdays. This function falls under the Date/Time category in Excel. It's commonly employed in accounting and finance to determine staff's benefits depending on days worked, the number of working days available during a project, or the business days needed to resolve a customer issue, among other applications.

The syntax for using the Networkdays function is:
=NETWORKDAYS (start_date, end_date, [holidays])

10.6.4 Days()

Calculating the number of days between two dates is made easy with the DAYS function. Using the formula =DAYS(end_date, start_date), you can obtain the desired result. Simply input the end date and start date into the function, and it will return the number of days between the two dates. This can be particularly useful for various applications such as project planning, determining the duration of events, or tracking the length of time between specific occurrences.

10.6.5 Counta()

The COUNTA function checks if a cell is empty. As a data analyst, you encounter incomplete data sets often. By using COUNTA, you can easily identify any gaps in the dataset without having to reorganize the data.

The syntax for COUNTA is =COUNTA(value1, [value2],...), where value1, value2, and so on are the values or cells you want to count.

10.6.6 Sumifs()

When working with data, the =SUMIFS formula is essential for analysts. While =SUM is common, what if you have to sum data using multiple conditions? That's where =SUMIFS comes in.

The syntax for =SUMIFS is straightforward: =SUMIFS(sum_range, range1, criteria1, [range2], [criteria2],...).

10.6.7 Countifs()

The COUNTIFS function in Excel is a robust tool for analyzing data. It functions similarly to SUMIFS, but instead of summing values, it counts the number of values that meet specific conditions. Unlike SUMIFS, it doesn't require a sum range. Its syntax is simple: =COUNTIFS(range, criteria).

10.6.8 Averageifs()

AVERAGEIFS, much like SUMIFS, helps you calculate an average using specific conditions or criteria.

The syntax for using the AVERAGEIF function is:
=AVERAGEIFS (avg_rng, range1, criteria1, [range2], [criteria2],...)

10.6.9 Hlookup()
The HLOOKUP function, short for "horizontal lookup," is denoted by the letter H. It is used to search for a value in the top row of a table or an array of values and then retrieve a value from a row specified in the array or table, but in the same column. This function is particularly useful when your comparison values are arranged horizontally across the top of a data table and you want to retrieve data from a specific row.

The syntax for the HLOOKUP function is as follows: HLOOKUP (lookup_value, table_array, row_index, [range_lookup]).

10.6.10 Vlookup()
VLOOKUP, short for 'Vertical Lookup,' is an Excel function. Its purpose is to search for a particular value in a column (known as the 'table array') and then retrieve a value from another column within the same row.

The syntax for the VLOOKUP function is as follows: = VLOOKUP (lookup_value, table_array, column_index_num, [range_lookup])

Conclusion

As we conclude our journey into the world of Microsoft Excel for beginners, it's clear that this powerful tool offers a multitude of benefits for both personal and professional use. With its user-friendly interface and diverse functionality, Excel provides an accessible entry point into the world of data organization and analysis.

By mastering the basics of Excel, beginners can streamline their daily tasks and boost their productivity. From creating simple spreadsheets to performing complex calculations, Excel empowers users to handle data with ease and precision. As beginners continue to explore its features, they'll discover new ways to visualize and interpret information, making informed decisions and driving success in various endeavors.

In today's data-driven landscape, proficiency in Excel is a valuable skill that opens doors to numerous opportunities. Whether pursuing a career in finance, marketing, or any other field, a solid understanding of Excel can set beginners apart and enhance their employability. Moreover, Excel's adaptability ensures that beginners can apply their newfound knowledge across different industries and disciplines, making it a versatile and indispensable tool.

As beginners embark on their Excel journey, it's important to remember that mastery comes with practice and patience. By embracing a growth mindset and seeking out resources for continuous learning, beginners can expand their Excel proficiency and unlock its full potential. With dedication and perseverance, they will build a strong foundation for future success by harnessing Excel's capabilities to their advantage.

END

Thank you for reading my book.

Jack A. Finke